JAMES LESEDI

THE PROSPEROUS COACH

The Ultimate Guide on How to Start Your Own Coaching Business, Get a Quick and Easy Guide on How to Establish a Lucrative and Successful Coaching Business

My Ebook Publishing House
Bucharest, 2021

TABLE OF CONTENTS

INTRODUCTION 7

Chapter 1. **Why Start An Online Coaching Business?** 9

Chapter 2. **Developing a Successful Online Coach Mindset** 16

Chapter 3. **Essential Steps For A Successful Online Coaching Business**............................ 24

Chapter 4. **Effective Delivery Of Online Coaching** ... 31

Chapter 5. **Setting Up A Website For Your Online Coaching Business** 39

Chapter 6. **Getting Clients for your Online Coaching Business** 53

Chapter 7. **Different Types Of Online Coaching Services You Can Provide**.................. 60

Chapter 8. **Best Platforms And Tools To Use For Online Coaching**.............................. 64

Chapter 9. **Successful Online Coach Best Practices**... 67

Conclusion 72

INTRODUCTION

If you have valuable knowledge in a niche that is in demand you can make a significant income as an online coach. A lot of people try to do this but they do not earn the income that they are looking for because they do not approach things in the right way.

In this guide we will show you how to start a profitable online coaching business. Because it is easy to start online coaching a lot of people dive right in and do not get the results that they were expecting.

You have to have the right mindset to be a successful online coach. Without this you are doomed to failure. We will show you in this guide the mindset that you need and how you can develop it.

Having a plan for your online coaching business is very important. Without a plan you will never know if you are truly *succeeding or not. We will show you exactly what you need to include in your plan so that you have the best chance of success.*

You need to make the right impression as an online coach and this starts with your website. There is no need to spend a lot of money on a fancy website. It just needs to be professional and we will explain what you need.

To make a healthy profit you need to attract the right clients. We have proven methods in this guide that will help you to find those clients. You will see that you have a number of options here. Some will require a small investment while others are free and will require effort on your part.

There are a number of ways that you can grow your online coaching business and we have some good ideas for you in this guide. We also provide you with details of some useful tools that will help you to manage your online coaching business effectively.

CHAPTER 1

WHY START AN ONLINE COACHING BUSINESS?

With the advances in technology you now have a number of different ways to connect with people across the globe. People that are looking for coaches of all kinds can now find them very easily online. They have the freedom to find a coach that will really meet their needs who they will get on well with.

There are many people looking for online coaches that have the knowledge and experience to help them. If you specialize in a niche that is in demand, such as digital marketing, then if you follow the advice in this guide you will not find it difficult to obtain clients. You need to keep them happy of course which we will discuss later.

Does being an Online Coach suit you?

Anybody can start an online coaching business today. That doesn't mean that it is a good fit for everybody. Do you have expertise in a particular niche? If so then you certainly qualify as an online coach.

There is no doubt that if you enjoy teaching others what you know then an online coaching business is a great way to do it. You can set your own schedule and work whenever you want to form anywhere in the world.

But you need to remember that you will always have to find new clients to make the whole thing profitable for you. There are different ways you can do this which we will cover in a later chapter. It is rare that finding a small number of clients will be enough to sustain a full time online coaching business.

There are a number of courses available online that will teach you how to be a successful online coach. You can even obtain certificates from professional bodies to back up what you are doing. Online coaching is a great business to be in but you need to be prepared to provide the highest quality service to your clients and make a significant profit at the same time.

It helps you to Grow

When you decide to become an online coach it will do a great deal for your own professional and personal growth. If you are an expert in your subject there is always more to learn and you will be committed to doing this so that you can provide your clients with the most up to date and useful information.

It is very satisfying to teach others what you know and to help them achieve their own goals. You will need to be a good communicator, and as you perform more coaching you will refine your communication skills. Dealing with all different kinds of people will open your mind and help you to develop as a person.

To be a good online coach you need to be disciplined and organized. If you commit to a coaching session with a client at a specific time then you have to be on time. You should plan out your coaching sessions to ensure that your clients get the best from them and feel like they have received a lot of value from you.

There is Good Money in Online Coaching

Online coaches charge hundreds if not thousands of dollars for personal coaching. If you are coaching several different people at the same time then you can charge on a per person basis which will bring you in a good amount of money.

Most people never turn what they know into hard cash. This is exactly what an online coach does. They are happy to provide their knowledge to others in return for a significant sum of money. Experts in the digital marketing niche can charge thousands for an hour of their time. The same goes for coaches in personal development and life coaching.

When you are starting out you will need to charge less than this but an hour of your time can still be worth hundreds of dollars. By providing personal one on one attention to individual clients they will appreciate this and will reward you handsomely for it. As long as you are providing good value people will be happy to pay you what you want.

Create your own Schedule

You decide when you will work. Obviously you need to be around when your clients are and if they are in different countries then you need to plan for the differences in time zones. With today's technology you can send out reminders to your clients and use the Internet for all of your coaching sessions.

It is fairly easy for you to tell your clients when you are available for coaching. You need to be flexible here and make yourself available to your clients when it suits them. Some of them may have full time jobs and only be available at evenings and weekends. What you can definitely control is the number of coaching sessions that you provide in a day.

Very Easy to get started

You probably have all of the tools that you need to become an online coach right now. A laptop or desktop computer and an Internet connection and you are ready to go. Some online coaches claim that they can provide online sessions when they are on the move by using a tablet device. This is not something that we would recommend when you are starting out.

Clients will expect you to communicate with them using a messenger service such as Skype, Zoom, Facebook etc. You could offer your clients the choice of platform for your sessions. All of these services are free and you can even record the sessions that you have with your clients (there may be a small charge for this).

Everyone has email so you can use this as another communications medium. We recommend that you setup Google Drive or some other cloud service so that you can share materials with your clients. If you need them to see video footage then this will often be too large a file to send via email.

Then there is texting. You can send text messages anywhere in the world for very little these days. If your client likes this form of communication then ask them for their phone number and provide yours as well.

We recommend that you go for the best Internet package that you can for your coaching business. It is also a good idea to have a backup service as well. If your Internet access is down then you cannot provide coaching sessions. This is not going to go down well with your clients so always have a backup plan.

With high bandwidth Internet access you can hold video calls and easily share your computer screen for demonstrations etc. Your clients will appreciate this as you are really helping them to learn what you know. Most people appreciate over the shoulder training.

In the next chapter we will discuss the mindset you need to become a successful online coach...

CHAPTER 2

DEVELOPING A SUCCESSFUL ONLINE COACH MINDSET

People often think that they need some special "insider knowledge" to become a successful and profitable online coach. This is not the case. What you do need is the right mindset to make a success out of online coaching.

You need to have the right plan and take the right action. Assuming that you are providing effective coaching sessions for your clients this is all that you need. If you were to analyze a successful online coach you would find that they have the following traits:

- They are confident
- They have clarity
- They have a mentality of abundance
- They are always positive

Basically successful online coaches have a magnetic personality. People are easily drawn to them and look forward to their coaching sessions with them. Take a look at Tony Robbins for example. He has to be one of the most successful coaches of all time. So many people like him because of his magnetic personality. He started life as a janitor!

Unfortunately there are a number of online coaches that do not succeed. This is because they do not have the right mindset for success. They do not exude confidence and as a result they take the wrong action. Clients are not confident in their ability to deliver what they need.

These coaches may be total experts in their niche. But this is not enough. If they do not have the right mindset to wow their clients then they are going to struggle. Successful online coaches never appear desperate for business (even if they are). They are always certain that they can get the right result for their clients.

The good news is that you can develop the right mindset to be a successful online coach. If you follow the advice in this chapter then you will be well on your way. So let's take a look at the mindset changes that you need to make to be a profitable and in demand online coach:

1. **You have to be Confident**

People that hire you as their online coach expect you to be very confident in yourself and your abilities. They see you as their mentor and want to look up to you. If you don't have the right amount of confidence then you are going to struggle to find and keep profitable coaching clients.

You need to be confident in the way that you look and when you speak. One way to identify weaknesses in your coaching delivery is to record yourself providing a fake session. Use a video recorder so that you can play everything back and identify problem areas. Do this alone at first and then you can find people that will provide you with honest feedback.

Pay particular attention to the tone of your voice and your facial expressions. How do you greet your clients? If they ask you difficult questions how do you respond? How is your body language during a session? Do you look attentive and ready to listen?

2. **You have to have Clarity**

This starts with you being clear about what a successful online coaching business means to you. We all have different definitions of success so you need to define your own and work out how this will look and feel to you.

There is more to being a successful online coach than just money. Some people that have a lot of money are not happy with their lot in life. So we recommend that you do not make money your sole focus with your online coaching business.

Think about how being a successful online coach means to you emotionally and spiritually. Once you know this you can practice it all of the time. There are many online coaches out there that make good money but are not happy. This is not a place that you want to be in.

3. **You need to think Solutions**

Clients will come to you as an online coach because they are looking for solutions to their problems. You need to have the belief that you can provide a solution to any problem that your clients have. When you are first starting out you may be hit with some questions that you were not expecting so you need to handle this in the right way.

Unfortunately if people are paying you hundreds of dollars for your time and expertise they are going to expect you to have all of the answers right away. If you don't know the answer to something then you need to provide a credible response such as "there are several ways that you could approach this".

What you want to do here is buy some time so that you can come up with the right solution. When you first engage with your client tell them that you are an expert and you are committed to finding the right solutions for them. Tell them that you may need to spend time after your call finding the most appropriate solution.

You can find yourself getting into a negative thinking spiral if you cannot provide the solution that a client is looking for right away. It is essential that you do not let this overwhelm you and always believe that you can find solutions for every problem.

4. Adopt the right Lifestyle Mindset

Because it is easy to get started as an online coach, a lot of people make the mistake of diving in head first and then end up working crazy long hours for very little money. We recommend that you come up with a lifestyle plan before you open your doors for business. There are limits to what you will do - working long hours for very little reward will soon grind you down.

Think about the return on investment (ROI) you want from your online coaching business. This is not just financial. You need to think about time freedom and satisfaction too. If you are a prisoner to your online coaching business then it is not going to last very long.

So think about the money that you want to make and also the free time that you want from your new online coaching business. Also think about what will give you the most satisfaction from being in this business. This could be helping others for example.

Once you have your lifestyle plan worked out you can then decide how you will operate your online coaching business. You can choose what you will deliver to your clients and when so that it supports the life that you desire.

5. **Be Goal Orientated**

You need to set yourself challenging goals if you want to be a successful online coach. Standing still is not an option - it may be easy for you to share your knowledge with the world but always be thinking about moving up to the next level.

Don't stay in your comfort zone or you will never realize your potential. You need to embrace change and different challenges. Think big and set big goals. If you get too comfortable then you can become complacent and your clients will notice this.

What other ways can you further your online coaching business? Can you turn what you know into a successful digital product that you can sell for a high price? Or what about a membership website where clients pay you each month to view training videos that you have made and learn from other resources?

6. **Be a Collaborator**

While it is possible to become a successful online coach on your own you are likely to achieve a lot more by collaborating with others. Having the support of a good network will have a significant impact on your ability to attract new clients and increase your income.

There are many different ways that you can collaborate with others. You can do a lot without having to travel anywhere. Find people that have authority blogs in your niche and work something out with them. Offer them a commission to advertise your coaching services. Write guest posts for their blog with a link back to your website.

You can also find influencers on social media that will promote your business. These people have large followings and can instantly connect with people that you could never find on your own. So have a collaboration mindset to really grow your online coaching business.

In the next chapter we will discuss the essential steps that you need to take to develop a successful online coaching business...

CHAPTER 3

ESSENTIAL STEPS FOR A SUCCESSFUL ONLINE COACHING BUSINESS

If you fail to plan you plan to fail. Have you heard that before? It is likely that you have heard it many times and the reason for this is because it is true. If you just jump in to your online coaching business it is not very likely to succeed.

In the last chapter we discussed how important it is to have the right mindset. So we are going to put that into practice now by helping you to strategize your online coaching business. You need a plan and it needs to be good. Here are the essential steps that you need to take:

1. **What do you really want?**

There is no such thing as a perfect online coach. You can spend months on Google trying to find the perfect way to launch your new online coaching business and you will not find the right answer. This guide will certainly help you but you need to ask yourself some important questions before you get going.

There are no shortage of online training courses that will cost you a lot of money. Although the content in these courses is likely to be high quality you can never guarantee that it will be the right fit for you. As a starting point ask yourself:

- What income do I want to earn each month?
- How many hours do I want to work on my online coaching business?
- What kind of contribution do I want to make in the world?

Write down full answers to these questions because you are going to turn them into goals. The first is your income goal, the second is your lifestyle goal and the last one is your contribution goal. When you achieve all of these goals you will have an online coaching business that rewards you, provides you with the lifestyle you want and fulfills you.

2. Identify your Target Market

To succeed as an online coach you need to serve your clients in a way that the market is not effectively doing so at the moment. You need to know who your target market is and what their pain points are and the problems that they have. It is important for you to align with their desires so that they are delighted to work with you.

When you are able to provide effective solutions to people you will become irresistible to them. They will happily pay you whatever you are asking. Providing the answer to their problems is what you need to be about so you need to know as much about your market as possible.

There are a number of ways that you can do this. You can look for conversations online to discover the problems that your target market are having. Your aim is to know more about your target market than they know themselves. Then just tell them that you have the answers that they are looking for.

Create a plan around this. Find out who your ideal clients are and find ways to identify the issues that they have. In a later chapter we will show you some great ways to find potential clients for your online coaching business.

3. **You need to Stand Out**

Until you are able to build a solid reputation as an online coach you need to stand out from the crowd. This is particularly important if you are going into a competitive market. There is nothing wrong with being in a competitive market - these tend to grow more than other markets do.

The best way to stand out from the crowd as an online coach is to deliver solutions that really make a difference to your clients. Make a commitment to develop an irresistible offer to them that solves one of their top pain points.

Use your creative mind here and offer the best way to fix their problems. This could be a series of one on one coaching sessions, a group coaching sessions for their employees, a series of training videos for company personnel and so on.

4. **Price your Services right**

Be committed to providing value to all of your coaching clients. When you have the solutions to their problems you are in a strong position and you can charge accordingly. Some people will try to knock you down on your price. We recommend that you avoid these people especially if they are "bargain hunters".

Never forget that the solutions that you provide can make a significant difference to your clients lives. If your recommendations will save a business a lot of money then never be afraid to charge a high price for your expertise.

5. **Take Action**

Don't be a perfectionist. You do not need a website that costs a fortune and takes months to develop. Your website needs to look professional and explain clearly what you do. Anything more than that is just garnish.

Being resourceful is far more important than having a fancy website. Think about all of the people that you know and tell them that you are launching your new online coaching business. If they do not need your services then they may know others that do.

6. **Setup a Support Network**

Being an online coach can be a pretty lonely business. One of the best things that we recommend you do is to find a good mentor or mentors. There will be times when you are stuck on a problem for a client. With a good mentor in place it can be a lot easier to come up with the right solution.

Did you know that most good mentors have their own mentors too? Well they do and it is because nobody knows everything. No matter how much of an expert you are in your niche there will always be something that you don't know or are unsure of.

Make sure that the people around you provide their support to you as well. The support of your spouse and your family is critical. It will also help you immensely if your close friends are supportive as well.

7. Scale your Online Coaching Business

Think of ways that you can scale up your online coaching business. Your focus here should be on providing you with more income and freeing up more of your time. Why not create online training courses where you will share your knowledge with others for a premium?

Another thing that you can do is to create an online community for your target market. Instead of them paying you for one on one sessions you can charge them a monthly membership fee to gain access to the community and its valuable resources.

- In the next chapter we will discuss the best ways to deliver your online coaching...

CHAPTER 4

EFFECTIVE DELIVERY OF ONLINE COACHING

The way that you deliver your online coaching to your clients does depend on your strategy. Some online coaches deliver to a number of people at the same time while others only offer one on one coaching. There are other online coaches that do both. Regardless of your approach there are common elements that you need to get right.

1. **Prepare for your Coaching Sessions**

It is essential that you are confident with your coaching sessions. If you are disorganized and just "wing it" then unless you are a master coach with bags of experience your delivery will not be perceived as confident to your clients.

Always bear in mind that your coaching clients are looking to you to provide answers to their questions. Your main objective must be as a solution provider that inspires your clients. When people are paying you top dollar for your advice they expect you to be on the ball and give them what they want.

With new clients ask them questions using email or through an online form to get a good understanding of what their problems and pain points are. Give yourself time to prepare for the coaching call so that you can research if necessary or speak with your mentors to come up with the best response.

There will be times when a client asks you a question that you can't answer. When this happens you need to respond positively and tell them they you need to look into the issue further to provide them with the best answer. You have to manage expectations here - your clients probably think that you have all of the answers already.

Prepare your first coaching session around what the client has told you about their problems. Using screen visuals is a good idea and will be well received so spend time getting these ready before your call. When you prepare everything beforehand it will give you the confidence to deliver the best possible coaching session.

2. Add Accountability to your Online Coaching

Your coaching clients are paying you for your advice and guidance so you need to have information prepared for them. It is also a good idea to create materials in coaching calls that provide a direct response to questions raised. Versatility is very important and it is not just about providing static materials.

When you are delivering your coaching sessions focus on planting a seed. What you are doing here is providing ideas at the "seed" level that will take root with your clients and then start to grow.

Online coaching is a two way street. The onus is on you to provide the solutions but you want the client to play their part as well. They need to take action against what you have discussed so introduce accountability into your sessions. Tell your client at the outset that they will need to be responsible for the agreed actions in your calls.

There are a number of good tools out there that will help you to provide this accountability. We will cover the best tools to use in a later chapter. Whatever tools you decide to use they need to be visible by both you and the client(s).

There are tools that offer a number of interactive elements such as goal setting, calendars and journaling. Use these to your advantage. It is essential that you keep track of the actions that you have agreed with your clients. This will include actions for you as well as actions for them.

What you want is a number of coaching sessions with a client for maximum profitability. It is pretty unlikely that you are going to solve all of their problems in one coaching session anyway, but when you have an accountability trail it will always prompt another session.

3. **Be Flexible over Session Times and Platforms**

If you live on the other side of the world to your client then you need to be flexible over times for coaching sessions. It is not ideal to perform coaching sessions in the middle of the night. But if that is the only time that your client has available then you need to make the sacrifice here.

We recommend that you have as many conferencing facilities as possible at your disposal. A lot of people will be happy to use Skype and there are apps available for you to record your coaching sessions which you must do.

Always tell your clients upfront that you will be recording the calls. Explain that you will play the recording back afterwards to pick up on the agreed actions etc. Tell them that you do not want to write notes as this will deflect your attention away from listening to what they have to say. They should appreciate this.

You can offer a copy of the recorded coaching session to your clients if they want it. Another good reason for recording your coaching sessions is that you can learn from your mistakes. Take the time out to go through all of your early coaching sessions and think about ways that you can improve them.

4. **Use Video Calling where Possible**

You want to create a strong connection with your coaching clients. One of the best ways to do that is to use video sessions so that they can see your face and you can see theirs. It is easier to pick up on visual clues during a coaching session than it is audible ones.

For example if you are discussing a high level concept you will easily be able to detect if your client is confused or is switching off while you are trying to explain something complex. You can straight away check with them to confirm that things are sinking in with them or not. It is never good for your client to leave a coaching session confused.

If you are coaching a group of people at the same time keep the numbers low (less than 6) so that you can monitor the reactions of the different clients. For group coaching you will need something more robust than Skype or the other messenger applications. You need to invest in a video conferencing platform.

Be sure to cover all your costs of using this type of platform in your pricing. Also make sure that you can record the sessions. If it is possible to record both video and audio then go for that option so that you can really assess your performance in the sessions.

5. Be Responsive outside of Coaching Sessions

None of your coaching clients are going to expect you to be available 24 hours a day. But they will expect you to respond promptly to any emails or other forms of communication that they initiate with you. Some online coaches choose specific times of day when they will respond to emails from clients.

While we are all for time management, we do not agree that it is a good idea to keep coaching clients waiting too long for a reply from you. We recommend that you respond to emails or text messages or any other form of communication from your clients as soon as possible. They will certainly appreciate that and will feel that you really care about them.

As an online coach your aim must always be to delight your clients. They are going to know people that you don't and if they are delighted with the service that you provide they will happily tell others about it.

6. Be Empathetic

We mentioned that online coaching was a two way street above and that the client has a responsibility to take action as well as you. If they are late delivering these actions then never try to ridicule them or get angry with them. You need to show empathy and explain to them that it is in their best interests to follow through with the agreed actions.

If a client wants to have a call with you late at night because they are struggling with something as a result of your coaching sessions, then unless it is completely inconvenient for you we recommend that you have that call.

Listen to what they have to say and ask questions. If they need a bit more time to complete an action then tell them that is fine. This is not school and you are not a teacher who is going to place them in detention for not doing their homework!

In the next chapter we will look at setting up a website for your online coaching business...

CHAPTER 5

SETTING UP A WEBSITE FOR YOUR ONLINE COACHING BUSINESS

Some people may tell you that you do not need a website to launch your online coaching business. We strongly disagree with that. The other thing that you may read is that you can use one of the free website platforms to setup a website at no cost. We disagree with that as well.

As an online coach you are going to be charging clients hundreds and later thousands of dollars for your coaching services. If you don't have a website then it looks like you are trying to do things on the cheap. When you have a free website it definitely confirms that you are a cheapskate!

You need your own domain name, web hosting and a professional looking website. There is no need for you to spend thousands on some fancy design. Your website needs to look clean and professional and that is all. It is not necessary to spend a great deal of time and money on it.

Some people are reluctant to have their own website because they do not know how to go about it. We will cover some of the basics here and there are plenty of good tutorials on YouTube which will provide the necessary details for you.

1. **Choose a good Domain Name**

Creating your coaching website starts with choosing an appropriate domain name. This is your unique address on the Internet. If your own name is unique name then you can use this as your domain name. If your name is John Smith or Mary Jones then this will not be an easy thing to do as the names will probably be taken.

You could go for JohnSmithCoaching.com or something like this. Or you could go niche specific with something like TheDigitalMarketingCoach.com. We have not checked that these names are available. You will need to check yourself using a domain registrar such as godaddy.com or namecheap.com.

As a general guide we would encourage you to go for a .com domain extension if you can get one. They are the most popular by far and recognized by Google and all of the other search engines. If you can't get a .com then look for a .net or a .org. You can also check out country specific domain extensions such as .ca for Canada, .com.au for Australia and .co.uk for the UK.

Our advice is to make your domain name memorable and as short as you can. This is not always easy to do as most of the good names have gone. But with some trial and error you should be able to come up with a good name.

2. **Web Hosting**

You need web hosting to make your website live on the Internet. It is a place where you will store all of the necessary computer files to make your website operational and available for all to see.

There are many web hosting companies to choose from. They will usually offer different plans and prices per month. You need to budget between $10 and $20 a month for your web hosting. It is unlikely that your coaching website is going to get a lot of website traffic (visitors) certainly not at the start. You can always upgrade your hosting later.

Examples of good web hosting companies are bluehost.com, hostgator.com and siteground.com. Make sure that the web host you choose offers a one click WordPress install facility and has a large amount of disk space and bandwidth. You will also want to add an SSL certificate to your website for security and a lot of hosts now provide this free.

Once you have chosen your web host you will need to connect your domain name to your hosting. This is a bit technical and most web hosts will help you out with this. Alternatively there are a lot of videos on YouTube that will explain how to do this.

3. Install WordPress

The next thing you need to do is to install the WordPress blog platform on your domain name. You can do this easily using one click software that most web hosts provide. Again if you are in doubt ask your web host to guide you through this step.

WordPress is a content management system (CMS). It is very popular and millions of websites use the platform. It is totally free to install and use WordPress for your website. You do not need to know any web coding to add content to your new website when you use WordPress.

What you will need to do is to choose a theme for your new WordPress site. The theme is the web design element of your site. It is how it looks and feels and it is important to make a good choice here.

There are thousands of free and premium WordPress themes available. There are themes made especially for online coaching businesses. Go to your favorite search engine and enter "wordpress themes for online coaching business" and you will get some good results back. Here is an example of a page that compares the themes https://athemes.com/collections/coaching-wordpress-themes/

You will need to log in to your WordPress installation and then you will see your dashboard. On the left hand side there are many options available to you. One of those is to install a new theme. Select this and then upload the theme file that you downloaded. Activate it afterwards and your new theme is ready to go.

Another advantage of using the WordPress platform is that there are many plugins available to enhance your website. A good example here is a contact form where people can send you a message and this will be delivered to an email address of your choice.

There are plugins for other things too such as search engine optimization (SEO), special forms (these are great for asking your coaching clients to fill them out and let you know what their problems are), legal pages and much more.

A lot of plugins are free to use and some are available at a premium. Here is a good page with recommended plugins that you should be using on your WordPress website https://www.techradar.com/best/best-wordpress-plugins

It is very easy to install plugins. Just log in to your dashboard and select the "add new plugin" option on the left hand side. You can then upload the plugin file or search for a new plugin that you need. Install and then activate.

There are many good tutorials on how to setup and use WordPress for your website on YouTube. This is not a technical guide so we will not include specific details here. WordPress really is the best platform to use for your new online coaching website so be prepared to spend a little time learning about it first.

4. **Pages and Content**

There are a number of important pages that you need to include with your new website and these are:

- **Home page** - this is the first page visitors will see when they type in your domain name

- **About page** - this is a very important page which tells visitors who you are and what you stand for

- **Services page(s)** - this can be one page or a number of different pages whichever suits your strategy. Here you will define the services that you provide

- **Contact page** - this is where a visitor to your website can contact you directly by typing a message and sending it to you.

- **Privacy and Terms and Conditions pages** - these are legal pages which explain how information that is provided by your visitors is managed. You can get plugins that will produce these pages for you automatically.

It is important here to make a distinction about pages and posts. A page is usually static. Once you have created the pages above you will not need to change them very often. It is a good idea to test pages out to see how well they are converting for you and then make any necessary tweaks to them.

A post is information that is related to your niche and provides value to your visitors. We recommend that you make at least one new post a week about your niche. So if you are a digital marketing coach for example you can write posts about:

- Social media marketing
- Search engine optimization (SEO)
- Email marketing
- Copywriting
- Driving website traffic

Obviously you do not want to give everything away in your blog posts. Use them as a hook to get visitors to contact you about your online coaching services. You need to provide value in your posts but leave some questions unanswered so that your visitors will be able to learn more once they become a coaching client.

The reason that you want to create regular posts for your website is that it provides a reason for potential clients to come back and visit your site again. It is also good for SEO as the more unique content you publish the higher your rankings will be in the search engines.

5. **Your Logo**

We strongly recommend that you create a unique logo for your online coaching business. If you are not a graphic designer then there is no need to worry. There are plenty of talented people that can design you a great logo for a few dollars over at Fiverr.com.

If you want to do this yourself then you do not need to go out and spend a lot of money on graphic design programs like Adobe Photoshop. Just head over to Canva.com and you can choose a logo style and make changes to it to make it yours. This is completely free.

6. **Email Opt In Form**

Not many people are going to visit your website and become clients right away. A great way to stay in touch with potential clients is to create an incentive for them to provide you with their email address so that you can follow up with them afterwards.

You can create a special report for your visitors that tells them how to achieve something in your niche. It is best to address one or some of the problems that you have identified your target market has. So for example if you are in the digital marketing space you could provide a report entitled "5 Ways To Grow Your Social Media Presence".

The trick here is to make the report enticing enough for the visitor to want to provide their email address to you. These days people are reluctant to give their email address as they know that they are going to receive promotional emails from you. So make your free offer as compelling as you can.

You will need an autoresponder service to deliver emails to your email marketing list automatically. Two good services are Aweber.com and GetResponse.com. When you are starting out these will cost you around $20 a month.

You can set up a series of emails that will be delivered automatically to your new email subscribers with an autoresponder. Space these emails out over a few days as nobody likes to be bombarded with these messages. It is important to use enticing subject lines so that your emails will be opened.

It is also possible to send a broadcast email using an autoresponder service. Maybe you want to let your subscribers know that you have a special offer for them such as a 30 minute coaching session for free. You can choose who receives this broadcast. It can be all of your subscribers or just some of them.

You can easily create an email opt in form (where the visitor enters their email address) with autoresponder services. We recommend that you have a professional cover image created for your report and again there are many people on Fiverr.com that can do this for you for a few bucks.

7. Video

Another thing that we recommend is that you create a professional video of yourself describing what you can do for your clients. These days people would much rather watch a short video than read a lot of text.

It doesn't matter if you are not happy to appear on a video - just get over this and do it anyway. Coaching is a personal business and prospective clients will want to see your face and hear your voice before they make the decision to become a client.

You can host your video on platforms like YouTube.com, Vimeo.com and DailyMotion.com free of charge and embed the video on your web pages. These websites get a lot of visitors so you may get leads this way as well. Video is a must these days especially for online coaches so be sure to plan out a good video script and shoot a high quality video.

If you need to pay someone to shoot the video and edit it for you then do that. It will be well worth the investment. Doing it yourself requires a high quality camera, possibly some lighting equipment (which you may be able to hire) and video editing software to make your video the best it can be.

8. **Social Proof**

You need to get some testimonials for your online coaching business and add these to your website. If you are just starting out you can offer to provide some free coaching sessions in return for a testimonial.

Social proof is very important for all businesses and particularly important for online coaching. Potential customers will be looking for social proof that you do what you say and will offer them a totally professional service.

The best type of testimonial is video. When you offer your coaching services for free to get testimonials ask your client if they will be willing to appear in a short video. As a minimum you need a photo of the client and their business name and website address in your testimonials. This all adds to the authenticity.

Create the best Website that you can

When you have your own domain name and website it shows potential clients that you are serious about your business. This is good for your mindset as well. You are not embarking on a hobby here - this is a serious business that will generate income for you.

Having a good website makes you a lot more credible as an online coach. It showcases who you are and what you can do for your clients. You can add case studies to your website that explain how you have helped others in the past and the results that they achieved. This is great for your credibility.

Depending on the type of online coaching services that you offer, some clients will want to sign up and make payments using your website. This is especially true if you offer online training courses. It is less likely to happen if you offer one on one coaching but still possible so be sure to provide this option.

We recommend that you use your website as a lead generation tool. You either want prospective clients to contact you using your contact form or sign up to your email list by offering a great incentive.

Also use your website to deliver great value to your visitors. You need to establish yourself as an expert and authority in your niche, so provide them with great content such as blog posts to showcase what you know and what you can do. With valuable content on your site it will be much easier to convert visitors into leads and then clients.

Make it easy for visitors to share your content on social media platforms by providing buttons for the various networks that makes this easy. Make your website work for you 24/7 by adding a call to action on all of your pages and blog posts.

In the next chapter we will discuss how to get clients for your online coaching business...

CHAPTER 6

GETTING CLIENTS FOR YOUR ONLINE COACHING BUSINESS

You have identified your target market and now have your website setup and ready to go. It is time to get some clients for your online coaching business. We are going to show you ways to do this online. It is all about getting your message in front of the right people.

There are many tactics that you can use to get prospective clients to visit your website which will then convert them into clients. These include:

- Writing articles / guest posts
- Sending cold emails
- Running ads
- Creating videos
- Using social media
- Webinars

Social Media Groups

If you are targeting business customers then the best social platform to find them on will be LinkedIn. Some people have had good results using Facebook as well so don't dismiss this altogether. If your target market is individuals (e.g. you are coaching people to make money online) then Facebook is the best social platform.

The reason that LinkedIn and Facebook are so good is that they have groups of people that are interested in different niches. A search on either platform will reveal the groups that are available for a niche.

So one of the first things that you can do is to join these groups and start posting some valuable content. People often ask questions in these groups or ask the group for help with a specific problem that they are having.

You can add useful posts to the groups as well. What you want to do is establish yourself as an expert in your niche as quickly as you can. People in the groups will definitely start to notice you when you are active and providing answers to questions and useful posts. A lot of coaches find clients using this method.

Pay Per Click (PPC) Ads

You can use Google or Bing to place pay per click (PPC) ads which are triggered by specific keywords. This can be a very effective way of driving targeted traffic to your website but you need to be careful with this as the costs can soon mount up.

If you like the idea of this method then the first thing you need to do is to conduct some keyword research. A keyword is the term that a user enters into a search engine when they are looking for something.

So for example they may enter the keyword "digital marketing coach" or "internet marketing coach". Use the free Google Keyword Planner to find the most appropriate keywords (there are tutorials on YouTube for this). Create a keyword list then set up a campaign with Google Adwords or Bing Ads.

You will only pay when a visitor clicks on the ad and visits your website. Once they are on your website it needs to convert the visitor into a lead by them contacting you or subscribing to your email list.

Social Media Ads

Most social platforms now offer the ability to run ads to drive traffic to your website. Facebook and Instagram are really good at this and LinkedIn are getting better. These social media ads tend to be cheaper than Google Adwords PPC ads and you can specifically target people which you cannot do with PPC.

There are all kinds of analytics available for social media ads that will tell you how well your ad is doing. You can choose who to target and in which locations. Targeting members of niche related groups is a good place to start.

Write a Book

One way to really establish yourself as an expert in your field is to write a book. This will require time and effort on your part but it will be worth it when you have completed the book. You can get a professional cover made for your book and distribute it on Amazon Kindle and other platforms.

Some coaches create a hard copy of their book and give these out at networking events etc. A digital version is a good place to start. You can promote the book on your website as well and even give some free copies away to get you started.

Guest Posting

The idea here is that you write a high quality article about your niche and then find blogs that are in the same niche and ask the owners if they will publish your post. Most blog owners are always on the lookout for high quality content to add to their blog. Some will even specifically offer guest posting.

You should be able to find related blogs that will accept your post. Some may charge you for the privilege, but if they get a lot of visitors then this can be a good deal for you. You need to add a link back to your website in the post that you publish so that the readers can find out more about you and what you offer.

Email Marketing

We talked about this in the last chapter. You will need to provide an attractive incentive for people to want to provide their email address to you and become a subscriber to your email list. Once they are on your list you can send them a series of emails, a few days apart, which provide value to them.

Email marketing is a very effective way to get coaching clients. But you must provide value in your emails. Of course you can tell them about your coaching services in the emails but do not use a hard sell approach otherwise people will unsubscribe from your list.

Creating Videos

A lot of people do not like the idea of creating videos but they are a great way to drive targeted visitors to your website. YouTube is the second biggest website in the world and it gets a ton of visitors each day looking for all kinds of content.

You could create a series of videos showing how to achieve something that is relevant to your niche. These kinds of "how to" videos are always popular. Don't give too much away in the videos but make it very clear that you know what you are talking about. Be sure to mention your coaching services in each video.

You can set up your own channel on YouTube. Each video that you upload needs to be properly optimized with the right title, description and tags (all based on keywords) so that YouTube users can find your video when they search. Add a link to your website on the first line of the video description.

YouTube is not the only game in town. DailyMotion and Vimeo are popular video sites as well. They do not get anywhere near the traffic that YouTube does but they still get a lot of visitors. Make good videos and spread the word.

Webinars

A webinar is an online presentation where hundreds, if not thousands of people can all watch at the same time. You can find someone in your niche that has a large email list and do a deal with them. They will send out an email telling their subscribers about your webinar and you will provide the list owner with a commission on all sales that you make.

You will need to plan your webinar so that it is the best that you can make it. Your presentation should solve a problem that people have in the niche and provide value. You will give away some of your secrets and then if they want more they will need to become a coaching client at a special discounted rate.

In the next chapter we will discuss the different types of online coaching services that you can provide to scale your business...

CHAPTER 7

DIFFERENT TYPES OF ONLINE COACHING SERVICES YOU CAN PROVIDE

There are a number of different ways that you can sell your expertise as an online coach. We will look at the most popular ways to do this in this chapter. You can start with one method and then scale your business by using the other methods.

One to One Live Coaching

This is one of the most popular methods of online coaching. A client agrees to pay you for a single session or specific number of sessions. You then agree dates and times with the client to provide the coaching using a platform such as Skype or Zoom.

Once you are established you can charge very high prices for one to one coaching. Some of the top experts charge $10,000 for an hour of coaching. Less established coaches will charge a few hundred dollars. A lot of clients like the personal attention from one to one coaching so are willing to pay a premium for it.

The biggest disadvantage of one to one coaching is that you are selling your time. But it is certainly worth doing if you can sell a short amount of your time for hundreds or thousands of dollars.

One to Many Live Coaching

This type of online coaching is popular in the educational market. Professors will teach a small group of students at once and take questions from them. You can do this for your business as well but the logistics of getting all of the clients together on the same day and the same time can be tricky.

If you want to pursue this type of coaching then you can charge each person a specific amount that will total a bit more than you would charge for one to one coaching. It is tougher to run these sessions than it is with one to one coaching and again you are selling your time.

Training Courses

The problem with live coaching is that you are selling your time. Yes you can make a lot of money with live coaching but another type of coaching that you can offer is training courses. A lot of people like to learn with online training courses. Websites like Udemy.com have grown significantly over the last few years.

It is going to take you quite a bit of time to create a high quality training course. If you want to charge a lot of money for your training then you will have to create videos. Nobody is going to pay you hundreds of dollars for a few PDF documents.

The good thing about training courses is that you can create more than one. Look at the problems that people are experiencing in your niche and create a training course that provides solutions to all of these problems.

You can sell your training courses from your website or you can use external platforms to host your videos and documents. Remember that the external platforms will take a fee from you for hosting your courses. Usually this is a percentage of each sale so check all of this out before you go ahead.

Webinars and Membership Sites

With a webinar you will give away some of your advice for free and then provide more information in a high ticket training course or through live coaching sessions. Webinars are more of a sales tool than a type of coaching but they work so well that we wanted to mention them again here.

You could create a membership site where people pay you a subscription each month to gain access to your live and recorded webinars. In these webinars you will provide the member with your most valuable information. You can also give your members other useful resources such as case studies, videos, documents etc.

In the next chapter we will look at the best platforms and tools to use for online coaching...

CHAPTER 8

BEST PLATFORMS AND TOOLS TO USE FOR ONLINE COACHING

There are a number of useful platforms and tools that you can use in your online coaching business that will help you to stay on track and be the best you can be. These are particularly useful if you want to provide live coaching sessions.

You do not need these to start with. It is possible to provide a great one to one coaching service using Skype and the free recorder tool that converts your conversations into MP3 files. You can also use the free Google Calendar to keep track of your sessions. We recommend that you use these tools once you have a few clients.

Satori

This is essentially an all in one coaching client management system. With Satori you get a business intelligence tool and a customer relationship management (CRM) tool rolled into one. The interface is clean and intuitive.

With Satori you can market your coaching programs (and even build them), use it for the distribution of proposals and agreements, generate leads, collect payments and make online bookings and send out questionnaires prior to coaching sessions. Satori starts at $39 a month.

Coach Accountable

You get a lot of administrative tools to run your online coaching business with Coach Accountable. This includes the scheduling of coaching sessions, payment collection, sharing documents and the creation of individual coaching plans. You can get started with Coach Accountable from around $20 a month.

Nudge Coach

Nudge Coach is an online coaching platform that you can fully customize. It will help you get clients and keep them and contains daily trackers that you can personalize for individual client requirements. You can also organize group coaching sessions with Nudge Coach and more. Prices start from around $25 a month.

Calendly

As the name suggests, this is a calendar application that will integrate with your existing calendar (Outlook, Google etc) allowing you to book sessions seamlessly. You can then send out booking links to your clients at dates and times you are available. This app makes you a lot more efficient with your session bookings. If you only run one calendar it's free.

Zoom

Zoom is a conferencing app used by a lot of online coaches. Your clients do not need to have a Zoom account to use the platform. All you need to do is setup a session and then send the join link to them via email.

You can record your sessions with Zoom and easily share recordings. There is also a webinar feature which works really well. Zoom integrates with most calendar apps and task management tools such as Slack. It's really good for coaching small groups. The "Business" plan is really good at around $20 a month.

In the final chapter we will look at the best practices for being a successful online coach...

CHAPTER 9

SUCCESSFUL ONLINE COACH BEST PRACTICES

Here are the 8 best practices that we strongly recommend that you follow to start your own profitable online coaching business. A lot of online coaches do not succeed but we believe that if you follow these best practices you will have the maximum chance of success.

1. Understand the Benefits

There are a number of benefits to starting an online coaching business. You can make very good money in online coaching and as your reputation strengthens you can charge even higher prices.

You have the flexibility to work from anywhere and work when it suits you. It is pretty easy to get started with online coaching and it will also help you to grow as an individual as you deal with more and more clients.

2. **You need the right Mindset**

You need to develop the right mindset to be a successful online coach. All successful online coaches are confident in what they do. They know what they want to achieve and are very goal orientated.

Successful online coaches are very positive in their outlook and they have an abundance mentality. Their magnetic personalities help them to attract clients to them. They also have a collaboration mindset and work with others to grow their business. They are solution providers and always think this way.

3. **Plan your Online Coaching Business**

You need to put an effective plan in place for your online coaching business and not just dive straight in. Start by be clear about what you really want by asking yourself what monthly income you want to generate, the hours that you want to work and the contribution that you will make.

Be sure to fully identify your target market and understand their pain points and problems. Create your plan around providing solutions to these problems. Find a way to stand out in the beginning, get your pricing right, create a support network and take consistent action against your plan.

4. **Deliver Online Coaching Sessions Effectively**

It is very important that you deliver your online coaching sessions in the most effective way. Avoid perfectionism here but be the best you can be. You must prepare well for your coaching sessions whatever type of coaching model you are using.

When you are providing live one to one or group coaching it is essential that you add accountability. Create all of the materials that you will give to your clients before the sessions. Agree actions on the session calls and document these for both parties.

Be flexible around your clients needs when it comes to booking coaching sessions. Always conduct video coaching sessions where you can as it is important that you see your client and they see you. Be responsive to any emails or other communications your client sends you outside of coaching sessions.

5. **Setup a Professional Website**

We strongly recommend that you setup a professional looking website. Get your own domain name and web hosting and use the WordPress platform for your site. Choose an appropriate theme and create all of the necessary pages which add credibility. Have a professional logo made for your online coaching business and use this on your website.

Provide valuable content on your website in the form of blog posts and videos. Create an attractive incentive that you will give away in exchange for the visitors email address so that you can follow up with them afterwards. Get testimonials for your online coaching services and add these to your website.

6. **Getting Clients**

Use a number of different strategies to find clients online. Look for Facebook or LinkedIn groups in your niche and become a member of these groups to provide value. Create PPC ads and test these for effectiveness on either Google, Bing or both.

Test social media ads on Facebook, Instagram or LinkedIn whichever fits with your target market. Check the analytics to see what is working and what isn't. Write a book around your niche to establish credibility. Write guest posts for high traffic blogs in the same niche. Create videos for targeted traffic and use webinars to sell your coaching services.

7. **Different Coaching Services**

There are a number of different online coaching services that you can offer to scale your business. One to one live coaching is very popular and you can charge high prices for this. You can also provide live coaching to a small group of clients.

You can create training courses for passive income. Video based training is best and you can charge the most for this. If you use a platform to sell your training courses they will charge a commission. Create a membership site where clients pay you each month to access valuable resources, weekly webinars and so on.

8. Online Coaching Tools

There are a number of useful tools available to you as your business grows. These are not necessary to start your online coaching business. Administrative platforms that help you to sell and organize your coaching sessions include Satori, Coach Accountable and Nudge Coach.

A good free calendar app is Calendly and this will integrate with your current Google calendar or Outlook. You can send out booking links directly from this app. Consider using the Zoom conferencing platform. This is excellent and you can record all of your sessions. Your clients do not have to have a Zoom account to use the platform.

CONCLUSION

We have worked hard to bring you this guide on creating a profitable online coaching business. The methods revealed in this guide are proven and will work for you if you apply them. Please do not just read this guide and do nothing. You are only going to create a profitable online coaching business if you take action.

In this guide you have everything that you need to launch and maintain a successful online coaching business. We have provided you with ideas on how you can grow your business as well and create passive income from it. Now it's over to you.

We wish you every success with your online coaching business.